CRAP

and grow rich

By Alan Gardiner

Published in the United Kingdom in 2014 by Leecroft Publishing, Poynton House, Shropshire Street, Market Drayton, Shropshire , U.K

ISBN 978-0-9928528-0-1

Foreword

I would like to thank some people who have had an influence in my life, firstly my parents. My parents are Anglo Indian. Born and raised in India but from British parents.

They came to the UK in the early 60's with just a pound in their pocket and suffered great hardship to give us a life of opportunity. They worked long days with rarely a day off for many years just to ensure we were housed and fed. We were rich because I was bought up in a home full of love. I am what I am today in great part because of Mum and Dad

I also want to mention my soul mate Christine, she is my partner my lover my wife and without her support I would never have got this far, she has stuck by me through dark days when money was scarce and the wolves were at the door, she always believed in me, she has never questioned my path and always encouraged me, without her my life would be empty and pointless. Thank you for always being there for me. I love you now, always and forever.

I want to say to my daughters Olivia and Elle how proud I am of them. They are strong in their beliefs and they approach their life with 100 % commitment. They have such high expectations, I know they will live their dreams and grow to be incredible women.

Paul Dubois my fellow Director, he has stuck with me for many years, he believed in the dream when many doubted, he committed when many faltered and we will now live a life most will only dream of because of this. You have my gratitude and thanks.

Simon Wright my rock, a man of faith and family. He inspires me to be a better person, as he too is a man of honour. Without him this book wouldn't exist. He came with me on this journey barely knowing me, he committed to the cause in blind faith. My life is better because he is in it. Thank you

There are many people at different stages of my life who inspired me to be more, who encouraged me on this journey, without their input at that time in my life I wouldn't be where I am today and I've wouldn't be on the path I am on.
Sharon Maslyn
Mike Howell
Simon Goldstone
Sharon Bellingham
Steve Foreman
Rose Desouza
Colin Gardiner
Debra Gardiner
The RAF Regiment

Finally I would like to thank Tim Parker who in addition to serving his country also provided the illustrations for my book! Thanks Tim

Thank you all for being there for me. I will be there for you.

Thank you x

Contents

Stop Wishing Your Life Away   8

Dream   10

Get Good   12

Association   14

Time Out   16

Stop Sucking Your Thumb   18

Failure Diseases   20

Set Goals   22

Investment   23

Start   25

Fun   26

Self Talk   27

A Winning Attitude   29

Why Not?   30

Make Memories   31

Avoid Negative People   33

Commitment   34

Failure   35

Important Stuff   37

If You're Going Through Hell? Keep On Going !!!   39

Support a Charity   40

Tell Your Parents / Family That You Love Them   41

Avoidance   42

Focus On The Money Making Activities   43

Build Pipeline Incomes   44

Have a Routine   46

Don't Be Afraid Of No's   48

Bury The Past   49

Avoid Pity Parties   50

The Deal   51

99% Loyalty is 100% Disloyalty   52

People of Character   53

Faith   54

Being Rich   56

Never Give In   58

Crap and Grow Rich

Alan Gardiner left school with no qualifications. He joined the RAF at the age of 18 and spent 10 years in the RAF Regiment which he truly loved and still does to this day. In that 10 years he never achieved one promotion. He met his wife Christine in the RAF. She was often asked why she went out with him as it was obvious he was going nowhere.

Alan got involved in network marketing and over 11 years recruited 1000s of people and achieved the leadership levels. He took this experience in to his sales career and found himself amongst the top performers, qualifying for 30 free holiday incentives during his career.

In 2005 Alan left the networking company after a bad experience with his sponsor, promising never to do it again and deciding to focus on his career. Two years later he was made redundant on the 15th December. He took a job out of desperation on half the salary he was on previously and found himself £10,000 overdrawn at the bank and with £10,000 on his credit card in a matter of months. He was on the edge of losing everything.

In 2010 Alan was listed number 283 in the world for top income earners in direct sales, he has built a multi million pound property portfolio and he has built a company in the Will Writing arena which is now one of the largest independent Will companies in the UK with assets running into millions. His Goal? To make his advisors wealthy in all areas of their life.

The principles of winning are out there, all you have to do is apply them.
Oh yeh, leave this book in the toilet then you can read it every day.
This book was originally written for Alan's sales advisors, the first step is to believe.

1. Stop Wishing Your Life Away

I was once asked the question 'How many days does the average person live for? More than 100,000 days or less than 100,000 days?' I thought MORE ..

If you live until you are 80 years old you have 29,200 days on this earth.

It's not a lot when you put it like that is it? How many times have you wished your life away? I can't wait till the weekend! Two weeks from now I'm going on holiday! Thank God it's Friday! Next weekend it's a bank holiday weekend! I CAN'T WAIT TILL ITS 5 PM AND I CAN GO HOME!

Yes I know, we are all guilty of it. We just wish our lives away, hour by hour, day by day. But with only 29200 days, how many have you got to waste? The answer is NONE.

You see life is to be enjoyed not endured and, trust me, there is always someone worse off than you. Now if you are that person, the person whose life is so bad there is no one worse off than you, then I have a solution - CHANGE.

If you hate it that much - CHANGE. Even if you are dying, do you want to spend your last days here miserable? Hey, trust me, we will all be joining you in the next 29,200 days.

Let everyone else feel sorry. You, my friend, have some dreams you need to achieve before you go.

If you have just lost someone you love, the last thing they would want is you moping around. You'll meet them again before you know it, trust me.

Live every day like it's your last, don't be too irresponsible, but don't be too responsible either.

Life is too short to be miserable.

2. Dream

I know, I know, every PMA book in the world covers this. Then if that's the case, why aren't you doing it? Anyone who has achieved greatness in their lives started with a dream. Sportsmen/women, pop stars, actors, all had a dream that one day they would be .... whatever. Even they had some thumb sucking non dreamer who did their best to talk them out of it - BUT THEY DID IT ANYWAY.

But a dream doesn't have to be 'I want to be David Beckham'. It could be to visit a place, to do a marathon, to help a charity, to do something special for Mum and Dad, to work towards your dream car, house, job or holiday.

No, seriously, why not?

Why couldn't you do it? Who told you you couldn't? The answer to that is easy, YOU said you couldn't. Are you going to procrastinate for your 29,200 days or are you going to get off your butt and do something about it?

You may have guessed by now I am not renowned for my diplomacy, but I do have a genuine love for life and people and if you want to do something with your life, and you need a kick up the backside to help you do it, then I AM YOUR MAN.

Get on with it, whatever it is. Stop giving yourself excuses. There is someone out there whose circumstances were a lot worse than yours who did it . Why not you? Plan it! Prepare for it! Have a strategy! When everything is in place - DO IT!

3. Get Good

'Get Good' means 'Get Out Of Debt'. There is a basic principle in life, if you spend more than you earn then you will be in debt and probably be miserable most of your life. If you spend less than you earn you will prosper.

How many times have we got things on HP, credit cards, store cards or simply gone overdrawn at the bank? I know I can talk on this subject with authority having made this mistake myself in the past.

The bottom line is, if you can't pay cash for it, you probably can't afford it.

Obviously we have the odd exception, like a house, but in real terms that new leather jacket isn't a priority in life. People generally buy on emotion. With this in mind, a good practice to learn is 'delayed gratification'. Buy it when you have achieved something worthwhile, set a goal for it, or simply delay the process of buying for 24 hours. Maybe this 'must have' item may not be as appealing after a night's sleep.

If you are in debt, the first thing to do is to get your accounts out and establish how bad it is. Work out the interest payable on each debt and the amount outstanding. Cut all extravagances, skin it to the bone, drop the £60 a month you're paying to watch rubbish TV, make your lunch at home, renegotiate your utilities with alternative suppliers. You get the idea, right? Give yourself a budget to live on and any excess funds should be paid into clearing your debt. I suggest the smallest amount first, as when this is cleared it will enable you to put more money towards debt clearance thus compounding the effect. If however you have no funds left, then it would make sense to seek professional advice. The Citizens Advice Bureau will be able to point you in the right direction.

The key is NOT TO IGNORE THE PROBLEM. Putting your head in the sand doesn't make it go away. Face it and deal with it .You will feel a 100% better when you know you are on your way to being Debt Free.

4. Association

You become what you associate with. If your child started hanging around other kids involved in drugs, would you like it? Why not? You have good kids right? You brought them up with the right morals and ethics didn't you? So why be nervous?

You are nervous because they could be influenced / tempted into trying it. There is nothing as powerful as association. It has killed dreams where they started and yet has given wings to dreams by others.

There are two kinds of people in life. People who make you feel good and people who make you feel bad. People either encourage and uplift or they discourage and put you down.

Question - Who do you want to associate with?

There is a theory that if you take the five people you spend most of your time with and add up their income, divide that total by five to get the average, then that number will be approximately what you are earning.

Who are you associating with? Family is family. I was very fortunate to have a supportive family, you might not be so lucky. Either way, you need to seek out a mentor. Someone who has achieved something with their life, who has the right morals and ethics and who is ambitious. Associate with people who are positive, HAPPY and who have goals and dreams.

You see birds of a feather flock together. Go to places where people like this go.

Pick your associates carefully, they form your mindset and in turn determine your outlook on life.

5. Time Out

Taking time out is vital. How many people have you seen who built tremendous careers only to find when they have achieved their goal they realised that they have lost their family in the process.

Spending every waking hour chasing your dream at the expense of your family and health is an unrewarding endeavour. Sadly the people who get caught in this trap are genuinely doing it for their family and yet lose them in the process.

Balance is the key.

Family time should be none negotiable. I have a good friend of mine who religiously will dedicate one whole day per month to each individual child. It's their day. A day where they have their father's undivided attention. He/She does not have to share their daddy that day. They go to the pictures, go shopping, play in the park, eat out, watch the sun go down and eventually star gaze as the day draws to an end.

I know some of you are thinking one day a month is not a lot !!

Well, tell me when was the last time you spent the whole day with just one of your children, or in fact spouse, without any distractions. It's a rarity today and yet shouldn't be. I am also not suggesting that one day a month is all that is required. You should ensure you have quality time with your family every day. I know that this isn't always possible, but it is a good goal.

It is also important to ensure you have time with your spouse and, in fact, time for yourself.

You see there is no job that important that I would willingly lose my family over. So get things into perspective. Take some time to smell the roses, wrestle with the kids, make love to your spouse, stand in the rain, watch some wildlife, see a movie, eat at a restaurant or eat chips in the park.

Time out doesn't have to cost money, but I do know it will make you more efficient at work and you will probably get more done.

One thing is for sure, you will be happier and so will your family.

6. Stop Sucking Your Thumb

Pull your thumb out of your mouth. Yes, you heard right! Stop your pity party and get on with it.

Bit harsh?

Yes it is.

But do you know that in the history of mankind, sympathy has never, ever resolved the issue. Never has it changed the situation and in fact most people giving you sympathy will not spend two minutes thinking about you after you leave.

There are of course minor exceptions in respect to family and close friends, but in truth the rest don't really give a damn.

I am not trying to make light of your loss, or your illness or your current situation, in fact I know there will be many people out there who are suffering. I know sometimes life is difficult but that is when you need to show your character.

That is where true leaders appear. In times of hardship you must get up, you must continue to fight and never give in.

So when you are up against it - GET UP.

It's never over till it's over

Make a difference in someone's life. Don't get into the hole with them, give them a hand to get out of the hole. Be an example to your family and the rest of your community.

Count your blessings and move on.

You can do it, it's only a decision.

Go on, do it - take your thumb out of your mouth.

7. Failure Diseases

There are lots of them but the three below are the worst.

Procrastination
Putting off till tomorrow what you can do today. Delaying the task/
event.
Procrastination is probably the main reason why the majority of people
live an unfulfilled life. They never get around to getting started.

So what's the answer? Just Do it !!!!!!!!

Get off your butt and do it now - I'm serious !!!!!

That's all it takes, a decision to start.

Detailitis
This is when you get so caught up in the details you never get started.
You want everything just right before you begin, you need to know
everything about a subject before you start, you tend to over complicate
things.

Yes I know you engineering/detailed type people are thinking 'I need to
have a basic idea of what I am going to do'. Yes you do! But there is a big
difference between that and requiring so much info that you never get
around to starting.

And finally

Excusitis
I know some of you are thinking 'that's not even a word'.

I'm not BOTHERED !!!!!!!!!!!!

Excusitis is a thin shell of truth stuffed with a load of crap.
Everyone at some point in their life has convinced themselves of why they couldn't do something.

I can't stop smoking now I am too stressed at work. Blah blah blah.
You can justify not doing anything, but only you know whether it is a genuine reason or not. Let's face it 99.9999% of the time it's not, but it's easier to convince ourselves it is.

Don't allow yourself the luxury of a crap excuse.

8. Set Goals

Oh no not you as well.

Sadly yes.

You see, 'the truth will set you free' and the truth is, without a goal, you are going nowhere. You need a goal for what weight you want to be or what income you want or where you want to live or ………

If you don't know where you are going you end up going nowhere. Goal setting isn't just for the corporate salesman struggling to hit his target, it's for every man, woman and child out there.

Goals need to be precise and, most importantly, have a date on them.

If you don't have a date on it, it is so easy to procrastinate (that should sound familiar by the way) and you never get around to starting.

But what if I miss my goal? Then I come over with a shot gun and shoot your knee caps.

NO !!!!!!!!! Nothing happens, you reset the goal and try again. But you will be closer to the end destination for having that goal and with persistence, tenacity and desire, the end goal will be yours.

9. Investment

When we talk about investment we naturally think of money, however, investment comes in different forms. You can invest your time as well as your cash. Sometimes you may take a job that doesn't pay well but it will help in the future. For example you may take a telesales role for a while if one day your goal is to set up a company selling a product. Selling of any form means you must be a skilled negotiator on the telephone, even if all you are selling at that point is the appointment.

Investing your time in attending seminars which will help you achieve your goal is probably a time and money investment. Don't be afraid to invest time or money in the education process. A recent two day course on property development I attended cost £3999, but one mistake in the property arena could cost me substantially more and the negotiating skills I learnt there have certainly helped me reduce the purchase price of property by tens of thousands. I think it was a worthwhile investment.

Now at this point there may be some of you thinking 'I haven't got £3999'. That's okay but there are other ways to get education. Network marketing businesses in some cases have incredible training systems. It was a training system like this that started my journey to Financial Freedom. I know that anyone who has been involved in a network marketing business for any amount of time will also be familiar with a lot of the principles in this book.

With access to a training system like this and application of what you learn, you are already learning the principle of investment.

Finally, you can't talk about investment and not mention financial investment/savings etc. Well this subject is massive and I recommend you read 'Rich Dad Poor Dad' initially by Robert Kiosaki and also 'Parable of the Pipeline' by Burke Hedges. These two books alone will help you understand the basic principles of money and I can assure you, once you have read them, life will never quite be the same.

There is a list at the back of what I believe to be recommended reading and audio programmes.

10. Start

Success begins with the word 'Start'.

The sad thing is most people don't. They accept their circumstances and live lives of mediocrity. I am not saying that just because you read this book that everything you try will work, that's ludicrous. I am also not saying that everyone is going to be rich. Life is more than money. Money helps but it isn't the only benchmark of success. I know many people out there that have tons of money and are miserable. Needless to say, I have met people in debt up to their neck and they are miserable too.

The people who are successful in life are the people doing what they love. If it's your dream to one day be a teacher and you achieve that goal and it is everything you thought it would be, then that to me is a success story.

You already know that you have dreams deep inside. May be it's to travel, then start planning and saving. May be a career change, then start planning how are you going to do it. Can you just get up and leave and start your journey? In some cases 'yes', in most cases 'no'. In most cases you might have to attend night school, do part time work etc but at least START.

My goal was 'Financial Independence'. No one owns me or controls me. I want to work when I want to work, play when I want to play, travel, spend time with my family and never have to worry about money again.

Whatever your goal is - START

11. Fun

Pretty straight forward this one - Have Some !!!

Life is too short to be miserable.

When was the last time you had fun?

You can be miserable or happy - it's your choice.

Go and play with your kids. When was the last time you had fun with them? If your kids are adults and working, play with your grand kids, nephews, nieces. Just go and have FUN.

Their Fun becomes your Fun. You'll increase your circulation and heart rate. You'll be healthier and happier.

What's your hobby you haven't got time to do any more? Make time. Get up an hour earlier, get the work done and go do it.

Join that club
Join that dance class
Take that holiday
Drive that car
Climb your mountain

Don't make excuses - Just do it!

12. Self Talk

You reap what you sow.

What you say is what you get.

So as you sayeth it shall come to pass.

These sayings are hundreds if not thousands of years old, they have survived this many years based on one fundamental. THEY ARE TRUE !!!!!

Our ancestors knew that what you say becomes a self fulfilling prophecy. It's been around since the beginning of mankind.

Have you ever noticed that there are some people that are always ill, they confirm and reconfirm this on a daily basis and so the brain ensures it gives them what they want.

Negative self talk reduces your belief, your attitude, your posture, the way you react to other people, in fact I can identify negative people within moments of meeting them. Negative people wallow in their circumstances and if you are not careful they will take you there too, in fact they normally attract other negative people. I have seen this many times in the corporate arena with disgruntled employees gathering together around the smoking area to moan how bad it all is, etc.

Positive self talk increases your belief, your attitude, your posture, the way you react to other people, in fact I can identify positive people within moments of meeting them also. Positive people adapt to their circumstances and if you are not careful they will take you there too, in fact they normally attract other positive people. I have seen this many times in the corporate arena. Ever heard 'birds of a feather flock together' ????

The last two paragraphs are virtually the complete opposite of each other. Let me ask you a question - which one would you prefer to live your life by?

One page is not enough to cover this subject, there are dozens of books and audios available in this area. Find them and apply them, it will change your life. I recommend reading 'What to Say When You Talk To Yourself' by Shad Helmstetter.

13. A Winning Attitude

Winners never quit and quitters never win. Winners ensure their attitude controls their circumstances opposed to letting their circumstances control their attitude.

They do not negotiate the price. They do not rationalise why they should not or cannot do something. They look for ways to succeed. They remain focused and positive in negative situations.

They are solution finders. They infect people around them. They inspire people to be more. They aspire to be more themselves. They dream the impossible dream but they also act on it.

They are also normal. Bad things happen to them too. They too can be a cancer victim, a victim of a tragic accident, a victim of the credit crunch, but they chose to approach their circumstances with an attitude of 'I will overcome this hurdle in my life'.

Does having a winning attitude guarantee that you always win? I think we both know the answer to that question, the answer is no. But what I do know is this - the chances of winning increases dramatically if you have a positive attitude and you believe you can. Sadly some people just give in.

I would rather live one day as a tiger than a lifetime as a sheep.

14. Why Not?

Many years ago, when leaving the RAF, I was looking for my next job. My mentor at the time was helping me achieve this. He told me to get the local job paper and circle all the jobs I was interested in, which I did.

When I got to his house we sat down and started looking at the opportunities I had circled. All of them were around the £12-£17000 a year bracket. When he asked me why, I explained I was currently earning £10,500 in the RAF and I wanted to earn more.

He then circled a job for £50,000 a year and said 'what's wrong with this job?' I told him I wouldn't get it.

He replied - 'Who said'????

I explained it was unrealistic and I wouldn't get it.

He replied - 'Who said'???

Eventually we got to the point and I discovered the only person who said I wouldn't get it WAS ME!!!!! So I applied, and, guess what? You're right, I didn't get it. But I did get a job with on target earnings of £40K and that year made £46K.

I learned my lesson. Why not me? Why can't I have that car, that house, that career, that holiday, that weight, that waist line? Why can't I stop smoking, drinking or anything else I want to achieve in life.

WHY NOT?

If other people have done it - why can't I?

Whatever your goal is - Why Not?

15.   Make Memories

Most people want to make a lot of money, have nice things and live in a nice house, but sometimes in chasing these goals we forget what is important. In my very early days in business, I was so busy making a living I didn't have time to have a life. In fact I missed the first five years of my daughter's life as I was so busy working I watched her grow up in bed. I went to work in the morning, she was in bed, by the time I came home, she was in bed.

When the Big Man upstairs says 'Hey Gardiner your time is up', hopefully when I am in my late 100s, I know I won't be thinking about 'I haven't finished the paperwork at work', it's more likely to be 'NOT YET!!! THERES THINGS I HAVEN'T DONE YET!!'
 I want to

Swim with dolphins
Do a parachute jump
Run a marathon
Stroke a tiger

Take the kids to Disney
See the Great Wall of China

In fact the list is endless! What do you want to do? What memories are you going to create?

My father, brother and myself went on Safari. We stayed at Treetops (the hotel on stilts where a young lady called Elizabeth discovered her father passed and she was to become The Queen). We got up early and watched the sun rise over the plains of Africa. It was beautiful. I saw a tear in my Dad's eye and the memory of that trip will stay with me long after he is gone.

You need to make memories with the people you love as you do not know how long they will be around. As you get older you begin to realise what's really important in your life.

16. Avoid Negative People

There is so much negativity in the world and some people thrive on it. I avoid these people like the plague. There are some people who are just sadly negative, they focus on what's wrong as opposed to what's right and they will be quick to point out why you can't succeed either.

Some of these people are sometimes disguised as friends. In fact they have a title, they are called 'Frenemies'. I recently had to explain to a colleague that a so called 'friend' was very jealous of her success in a certain endeavour and her friend took every opportunity to snipe at her. She didn't like her having other friends, she joined all her classes and continued to belittle her at every opportunity. She just basically had to be better than her in all activities. The strange thing is that my colleague was literally in a different league and this woman couldn't compete and deep down knew it.

The sad thing is my colleague was influenced by this negativity and started to question her own ability! Don't walk away from these people .... RUN.

Sometimes well intentioned relatives will be negative of your endeavours. Just be strong enough to understand in most cases they are not being nasty, they are just trying to protect you, but they do not necessarily know what you know.

Be careful who you allow to influence your life. True friends encourage, build confidence and support you in whatever direction you pick in life. These people are like gold, cherish them as they are a rare breed.

17. Commitment

Nothing happens without commitment.

Commitment is the difference between success and failure, winning and losing.

Olympic athletes train for four years to compete in a race that sometimes can last less than ten seconds. Rain, sleet or snow, these Olympians train even when they do not feel like it.

Even when they do not feel like it.

Did you read that?

Even when they do not feel like it.

You see committed people do the things that the none committed will not. There have been plenty of times in my life where it would have been really easy to back out of a commitment but I didn't. You shouldn't either. Most people pick and choose what they would like to do and avoid the uncomfortable. If you are committed to your cause you do what it takes.

Commit to your wife/husband
Commit to your family
Commit to your career
Commit to your calendar appointments
Commit to your workouts

If you haven't got it yet …….. COMMIT!!!!!!

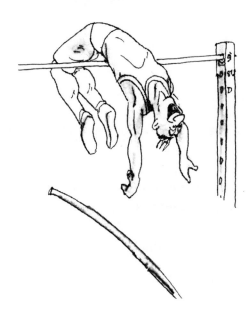

18. Failure

Failure doesn't mean Stop!!

I will say it again.

Failure doesn't mean Stop!!

The only people who don't fail are the people who don't try anything. So actually failure can be good as long as it's not the last time you are gonna try.

Let's talk about Olympians again, let's talk pole vaulting.

A pole vaulter will try time and time again to clear the bar and he nearly always knocks it off but he keeps practising over and over and over again and after many months of commitment, guess what?

He learns to clear it. Yayyyyy!!!!

Now guess what he does next?????

Yep, he raises the bar again and starts failing all over again. He just fails his way to success.

So in summary, failure is acceptable as long as it's part of the journey to success.

Failure is not the destination, it is just what you will have to experience at times in your life to help you grow as a person.

So if you have failed to stop smoking, try again.

Failed to lose weight? Try again.

Failed to get a job? Try again.

Failure doesn't mean stop.

19. Important Stuff

1. Cherish your Partner
2. Cherish your Children - they are not with you for long
3. Cherish your Parents - they age quickly and one day will be gone
4. Cherish your Friends - they will help you in this thing called life
5. Look after your health - life is not as good when you don't have it
6. Look after your knees - you will miss them when they are gone
7. Look after your finances or someone else will, this rule also applies to number one
8. Take plenty of photos and video - they will remind you of happy times
9. When you look back at these photos you will realise you were not really that fat
10. Enjoy your holidays - painting the house does not qualify
11. Enjoy the sun but use sun screen
12. Don't smoke - it will kill you in the end
13. Be faithful - if you can't you're on the road to nowhere
14. Work hard - it makes you feel good
15. Bumming around is for bums
16. Shower often - pigs don't know pigs stink
17. Credit cards should be cleared at the end of the month. If you can't then cut them up now before it gets worse
18. If you cannot pay cash for it you cannot afford it
19. Plan for your retirement - time goes quickly
20. Don't be afraid to tell the one you love that you love them
21. Realise everyone makes mistakes, try and be forgiving, one day it may be you needing forgiveness
22. Eat less or eat more - you know which one applies to you
23. Sleep...................
24. Set up a separate account to pay your bills and set them all up on monthly DD. It makes life easy and you will learn what your outgoings are in the process
25. Spend less than you earn
26. Speak good things and good things happen
27. You reap what you sow

28. Think before you speak - once it's said it's difficult to take it back
29. Love your work - it makes the day go quicker
30. Build not destroy
31. Love not hate
32. Do not miss the school play - it's important
33. Tell your kids how fantastic they are - no one else does
34. Breathe, no seriously. Stop and take a deep breath outside, fill your lungs
35. Make your Will
36. Make your bucket list (things to do before you kick it)
37. Pin this up in the toilet - I know you will see it every day
38. Before you take advice from someone, see where their advice has taken them

20. If You're Going Through Hell? Keep On Going!!!

The last thing you want to is stop there!!

There are some great books out there on this subject. 'Tough Times Never Last, Tough People Do', by Dr Robert H Schuller' is a fantastic read for people who are going through big challenges in their life. It's important that you understand that this is just a phase you are going through. It will pass with time.

I have suffered with the loss of a loved one, hard times financially, hard times at work and at the time it hit me hard. There were times I wanted to put my head in the sand and just retreat from life. But I was told all things will pass, even if you have a terminal illness it will pass one way or another!! But if we are only here for a short time then it makes sense to live our lives the best we can.

So just trust in the fact all things will pass. If it's tough now it does not mean it will always feel like this. Time is a great healer, but fighting through the crap means you get to the other side sooner.

Keep the faith, never give up, find your inner strength and keep on fighting and know that things will get better. Believe it will and it will.

Feel the sun on your face, take a deep breath and know that today is a new day.

21. Support a Charity

If you can't support it financially, then support it with your time. Do it without the need for recognition or payment. Commit to it long term. Help those that are less fortunate and, trust me, there is always someone less fortunate.

As a company we donate 5% of our company profits to charity. The MD of GWT tithes 10% of his income to his charity and church. I believe in karma. If you help people in your life, good things will happen for you.

Knowing that you have selflessly helped another human being, with no recognition for your deed, is not only very admirable but it makes you feel better about yourself too. It improves your self image, it helps the charity and helps the individual.

Find something that touches your soul, that gives you a sense of achievement.

And here's that word again, COMMIT TO IT!

You will be a better person for it.

22. Tell Your Parents / Family That You Love them!

I wish I could put loads of paragraphs in this section, but the principle is very straight forward. Most people die having never been told that they were loved. The regret of not telling that person you love weighs heavy on your mind once they have gone.

Do not carry that burden with you, tell your parents and your kids how important they are to you. I can remember telling my Dad for the first time that I loved him, there was an awkward silence and eventually came the response, 'Is everything ok?'. Northern blokes are not free with their feelings, expressing their emotions is difficult for most men.

Since then he has learnt to free himself from these emotional bonds too.

My Pops knows I love him and I know he loves me. My wife and daughters know how much they mean to me and we are not afraid to share our feelings.

23. Avoidance

One of the key reasons people do not make money is they avoid doing the things that they feel uncomfortable with. Successful people just do it. There are plenty of things in business I do not like doing but if I don't do them, I know I will inevitably fail. So guess what?

I DO IT!

Unfortunately most people don't. They will occupy themselves with other business activities that help them avoid doing the uncomfortable.

Key avoidance areas are:

Sales phone calls
Goal setting (if you set a goal with a date on it, you have to start working now)
Appointments
Promoting their business verbally to all they meet

Whatever it is you are avoiding, and you know what it is, have the discipline to do it. If you are not very good at it, you will not get any better at doing it by avoiding the task. You will only learn to master this task by repetition.

Stop avoiding it, do it now.

24. Focus On The Money Making Activities

I recently had a meeting with one of my consultants who asked for help in making his business work. He explained that there were so my avenues to go down in his business he was attempting them all but failing in most. Consequently he was getting into financial difficulty.

I asked him to write down all the areas to make money within his business. He wrote down six areas. I then asked him to list those areas in order of priority where he is spending most of his time.

Once he had done this, I asked him to do the same list again but write down in order which areas pay out the quickest.

What we found was most of his time was spent chasing the big deals. The problem in his case was that this was a long sales process which could take months. That doesn't pay the mortgage next week.

The area which paid out the quickest was number six on his list and was actually getting the least amount of time devoted to it.

We prioritised his list on the activities that have the quickest turnaround time to produce income. We spent more time in these areas and subsequently the cash-flow increased. Now it didn't mean he dropped the big deals altogether, he continued to progress this side of his business but he was more selective and managed his time accordingly. He focused on his bread and butter business and things turned around.

25. Build Pipeline Incomes

My mentor recommended reading a great book by a guy called Burke Hedges called 'Parable of the Pipeline'. YOU NEED TO READ IT!

The principle is to create five pipeline incomes. A pipeline income is an income that pays out month in, month out after you have created it.

For example:

Property - if you own a property and rent it out for £650 a month, that £650 a month comes every month whether you stay in bed or not. Now it will require work in the first instance and may require effort occasionally to find a new tenant or maintenance but in general once it's been set up it provides a residual cash-flow.

I invested in a call centre and have a share in it, my business partner runs the show and I refer business to it when the opportunity arises. But in this instance it produces positive cash-flow in to my account every month.

Within my Will Company we have partnered with a building and contents company that pay residual commission for every customer you introduce. The same applies to life assurance and storage facilities for the Wills we provide.

In fact I have helped/invested in lots of other projects that produce positive cash-flow into my account every month.

Did everything I invested time and money in work?

NO! But I persisted until I found the ones that did. The key is to develop five pipeline incomes that produce positive cash-flow into your account every month. Now if you lose a pipeline, you still have four others to carry you until you replace it.

READ THE BOOK! YOU WILL BE GLAD YOU DID!

26. Have a Routine

Having a routine is a massive part in successful people's lives, especially around health, family and business.

I train my advisors to have a weekly routine, for generating data, making calls and sitting appointments. I call it the Five Step Pattern.

The Pattern:

STEP 1 IS GOAL SETTING

a. How much do you want to make? £4000
b. What is your average commission per deal? £500 (therefore you need 8 deals to make £4000)
c. What's your conversion from sat appointments to deal? 100%
d. To get 8 deals how many appointments will you have to book? (Let's say 12 appointments booked, on average 4 cancel and therefore 8 sit)
e. How many calls to get an appointment? 6 calls to get 1 appointment
f. How many data records do you need to get your monthly appointment target? (12 booked appointments x 6 Calls) = a requirement for 72 data records per month

Therefore 72 calls = 12 booked appointments. On average 4 will cancel and you will sit 8 appointments = 8 deals = £4000

STEP 2 COLLECT THE DATA REQUIRED TO MAKE THE PHONE CALLS

You will need enough names and numbers to hit your monthly goal.

Based on the above target you will need 72 people to call per month. Where are you going to get your records from?

STEP 3 MAKE THE CALLS

When you make your calls it should be a set day and time,

e.g Sunday evening between 5pm & 8pm.

No distractions, you are there to book appointments.

12 appointments booked = 8 sat.

Therefore that's 3 appointments a week and on average 1 will cancel = 2 sat appointments a week.

Therefore 3 appointments = 18 calls per week (6 calls to book 1 appt)

STEP 4 SIT APPOINTMENTS

In your goal setting session your manager would have helped you decide where you are going to fit the appointments in your schedule. It is important that you make this a regular routine. You know that Sunday nights you make your phone calls and let's say that you will do your 3 appointments .... 2 on a Wednesday and 1 on a Thursday.

STEP 5 FOLLOW THROUGH

Ensure the client has a brochure and a business card should they have buyer's remorse.

Consider going back to help with setting up the service and gain five referrals.

27. Don't Be Afraid of No's

I was taught very early in my sales career getting a 'Yes' is easy, it was handling the 'No's' that was tough. I was told that there are 52 cards in a pack, but there are only four aces. Therefore how many cards would you have to flip to guarantee you would get an Ace? Well, they could be the last four cards in the pack so the answer is 48. It could come sooner but to guarantee you get one you must turn over 48, but remember every time you turn a card you are one closer to the Ace. You are one step closer to a positive result.

I used to target myself on 52 attempts, be it telephone calls, door knocks, cold canvass and I learned to enjoy the 'No's', they just became part of the process. I didn't go through the emotional roller coaster anymore as I accepted they were part of the process I had to go through to become successful.

Now here's the key, if you get 4 yeses early, DON'T STOP TILL YOU HAVE DONE YOUR 52 CALLS. The consequences of this may result in doubling or even trebling your yeses

What if I only get one yes out of 52? Well if you had a deal a day in most sales environments it would make you a successful salesperson. Now a hit rate of 1 in 52 doesn't sound great does it? But that would depend on how long it would take to get 52 responses, if it took a day, that's a result! If it takes you a month, then that isn't.

Read the book 'Go For No' by Richard Fenton' it's a fantastic book that goes into this subject in depth.

This principle doesn't just apply to sales by the way, it applies to job applications - even dates.

28. Bury the Past

Before it buries you. Past failures are part of the growing process, it's important that we learn from them but what we cannot do is live the rest of our life in fear of them. We cannot keep bringing them up as an excuse not to try again.

I read once that a car has a big windscreen and a small rear view mirror because it's more important to see where you are going rather than where you have been.

Your body doesn't live in the past - don't let your mind. There are many regrets I have with my life, people who I trusted who let me down, but these experiences drove me, they made me wiser next time round.

Whatever mistakes you have made in the past are in the past, leave them there. It's done. Move on, you change the things you can, you accept the things you can't and then FIDO -

Forget It, Drive On.

Make a commitment today that this is a new start, that today is the beginning of a new life for you, everything that you want out of life is there for you.

29. Avoid Pity Parties

As the task ahead gets tough and, trust me, it will, it always does, people will have a pity party, in fact they will try and invite everyone they know to join it. They will wallow in how bad things have become and they will confirm to each other "it's not their fault". Every success story is the same - Dream, Struggle, Victory. Without a struggle there can be no victory. Sadly not everyone will finish the game, some people quit. But interestingly enough they very rarely look at themselves as the reason for failure, it's always easier to blame someone else. My manager didn't help me, the company didn't support me, there's a recession.

Well this is sad but I accept it, it's a fact some people don't have the gumption to finish the task. The problem is they want other people to join their pity party, it makes their reason for failing acceptable. It's not my fault! It's theirs.

Let me tell you in every company I have worked for there was a group of people who flocked together to discuss how bad things were. They were always talking about how bad things were, in the meantime the top performers were just getting on with it, winning new business and all the holiday incentives.

Strangely how many in the pity party do you think qualified for these free trips? Yep, you're right, they were never there. In fact they didn't last long in the company, they didn't last long at any company.

Just remember, misery loves company, make sure it isn't you. These type of people go from one company to the next, never achieving anything anywhere.

30. The Deal

In a world where people are obsessed with wealth, we forget how fortunate we are. The British Forces enabled our freedom in the 1st and 2nd World Wars and continue to protect us to this day. It's because of this freedom and where we were lucky to be born that we have the opportunity to chase our dreams.

So many children in the world are dying because they do not have something as simple as clean water. There are children begging just to buy food. As you start applying these principles and you find yourself increasing your personal wealth, there is only one thing I would like you to do.

I want you to sponsor a child. Action Aid can help you sponsor a child and enable this child to be fed, watered and educated for as little as £25 a month.

Remember, I want you to do this when you start to reap the reward of your actions. We are judged in life by not what we have but what we do. Do something great with your life, impact the life of another in a positive way, uplift people, help them believe they too can make a difference. This isn't just about you anymore, this is about making a difference.

31. 99% Loyalty Is 100% Disloyalty

99% loyalty is 100% disloyalty. Let me ask the ladies in a relationship, if your partner was loyal to you 99% of the time but just one day a month he/she went off with another woman/man, is that okay with you? Is that acceptable that you partner is only disloyal occasionally?

The same applies with the people I work with, they get 100% from me and I expect the same in return. How many times does a person have to lie to you for you not to trust them? Generally once. Once you discover what they said was a lie, you second guess everything they say. Was that a lie or were they telling the truth that time? You can't build a business if you can't trust them.

So 99% loyalty is 100% disloyalty.

32. People of Character

We live in a world where we have instant coffee, microwave food and credit cards and get what we want in a hurry so it's sometimes frustrating when the results you wanted do not happen straight away. Life has a way of testing people's resolve, life tends to throw crap at you occasionally, but the true character of a man or woman is how they deal with that crap. It's all too easy to give in, throw in the towel or justify not continuing to strive forward (forge ahead). But some people persist, they dig deep, they know deep down that the endeavour is worthwhile; it's these people that inevitably win in the long run.

Strangely, when they do start to win, they are identified as lucky, people even say things like 'it's okay for them'. But these people have no understanding of the journey you have taken to get where you are. They do not realise that you also fought through personal problems but you persisted and you fought and eventually you won.

We all have doubts about the path we take sometimes. It's at these times that our resolve can be swayed by well meaning family or friends. It's at these times that your character carries you through. It's your character that keeps you honest, straight and true.

People who have character have things like integrity, commitment and belief. They commit themselves to a cause bigger than themselves.

People of character always come through. In times of struggle remember who you are and the team you are part of. Know that we are people of character and we always come through.

We are unstoppable and the world is our oyster. Your time in the sun is just around the corner.

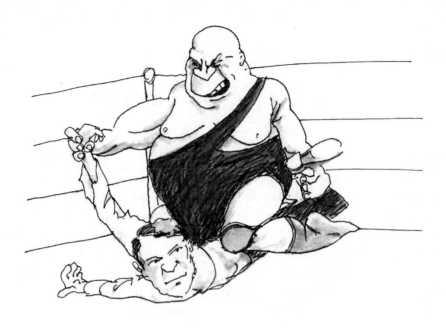

33. Faith

Definition:

1) Confident belief in the truth, value, or trustworthiness of a person, idea, or thing.
2) Belief that does not rest on logical proof or material evidence.
3) Loyalty to a person or thing; allegiance: keeping faith with one's supporters.
4) The theological virtue defined as secure belief in God and a trusting acceptance of God's will.

Without faith nothing is achieved. Without faith, people quit. Without faith they won't even try, you need the faith that you will succeed. Sometimes you need the faith to follow someone down a certain path. One of my closest friends is a Christian, his faith and belief is none negotiable. His faith inspires me to be a better person. He also keeps me honest and true. I may not follow the same path, but I take great comfort in knowing his faith supports my belief system too. That if you live a good life, then good things will come to you.

I am not of the doctrine that my God is better than your God, I also have no issues how you celebrate your faith, Catholic, Protestant, Muslim, Buddhist or any other faith, I take great comfort in how I live my life with my faith and I respect how you live yours.

But faith is vital in life, I have faith in my wife and she has faith in me, I have faith that my team will stick together in good times and bad. I have faith that any bad times will pass, I believe life is a pale shadow without faith.

If you have no faith in your partner, God, yourself or the leaders you are following, then where are you going? Most people I meet without faith are generally not chasing a goal or dream, they have no faith they are going to achieve it, they are wandering generalities.

There's another ingredient to add to faith in order to live a fulfilled life, you need FAITH & ACTION. I met a guy once who prays every night that he was going to get a Bentley, but takes no action to get it, he expects someone to give him one. I think he could be waiting a while. Yet faith and action are an incredible combination, I think if you have faith and action then you will achieve great things in your life.

Don't be afraid to express your faith, it's a commitment to what you believe in.

34. Being Rich

So what does being RICH mean? Making a lot of money? Today it has a bigger meaning. There are many examples of rich people who are extremely unhappy. Witney Houston and Michael Jackson are just two examples of people who had it all and yet their lives were unfulfilled and in turn they resorted to drugs. I know of many business people whose obsession with wealth and work cost them their family. They were so busy chasing the dollar they neglected everything else. High blood pressure, stress, strokes, divorce, no relationship with their kids. What's the point in making it if the consequences are so dire? Well the truth is there are people out there who got it right. They became successful and stayed healthy and kept the love of their family. Are they just lucky? Generally no! They made an effort to have balance in their lives.

As I write this chapter, my wife and family are sound asleep in bed as I enjoy a cup of coffee and share my thoughts with you. It's a beautiful morning and I'm going to walk my dog 'Beau' when we are done. I exercise regularly and spend quality time with my girls, I am truly blessed.

My company sponsors a Charity called 'Bethany's Wish', check out their website and read Bethany's story. Sadly Bethany lost her fight against cancer before her life had really started. Her parents took their pain and loss and turned it in to a charity to support other children with the same cancer as Bethany. I am grateful that my family and I have our health, we are truly rich.

You have to understand that if you have your health and family and you are fulfilled in your work and faith then in my opinion you are already rich. Being rich is no longer about just 'having money', it's about balance, without balance in all these areas what's the point?

What's the point in reaching your goal but as a consequence you have had a stroke, you lost your partner, you lost your family?

Being rich in all areas of your life is achievable with thought, care and planning.

35. Never Give In

So we come to the closing chapter of the book, what words of wisdom can I share that justifies being the last chapter of the book that could change your life forever. Well as you can see, I've entitled this chapter 'Never Give In'. When I was first dating my wife Christine many of my so called friends on many occasions tried to derail our relationship by telling her that I would amount to nothing, obviously trying to become my replacement in the process.

I had a reputation for being a hot head, which is never a good thing in the military. I left school with no real qualifications to talk of and yet I always knew I would do something with my life. As a child I always wanted a Porsche. Many people tried to tell me I was living in cloud cuckoo land and that I would never achieve my goals. Well these people far from demoralising me became my inspiration. They made me more determined than ever. They built a fire inside of me that has never gone out.

I want to thank them for their words of inspiration, without them I'm not sure I would have made it. I know that my English may not be correct, that I may not be as eloquent as some of the other 'Positive Mental Attitude' writers out there; I'm just a normal guy from a working class background that never gives in.

My life today is a life of wonder, I now get to travel and enjoy the fruits of my labour, I have had my Porsche, Mercedes, BMW and Audi. Next on my agenda is a Bentley and Aston Martin and why not? I have worked hard for it, diligently pursuing my goals against all the odds.

I love my life, I love my wife, I love my family and I love those with whom I associate. You see I'm surrounded by winners; consultants who became my friends and, just like me, they believe that most things are possible if you 'Never Give In'. I have my health and wealth.

Don't you ever give in, never surrender, fight till you breathe your last breath. Remember when you are in your darkest hour and at your lowest ebb that there's a bloke out there called Al Gardiner and he believes in you. Just drag your ass up and go one more time. You have one life to live, Live it and...........

Never ever give in.

X

"It is not the critic who counts; not the man who points out how the strong man stumbles, or where the doer of deeds could have done them better. The credit belongs to the man who is actually in the arena, whose face is marred by dust and sweat and blood, who strives valiantly; who errs and comes short again and again; who knows the great enthusiasm, the great devotion, who spends himself in a worthy cause, who at the best knows in the end the triumph of high achievement and who at the worst, if he fails, at least he fails while daring greatly. So that his place shall never be with those cold and timid souls who know neither victory nor defeat."

Theodore Roosevelt

Recommended Reading

Title:	Author/s:
Go for No	Andrea Waltz & Richard Fenton
See You at the Top	Zig Ziglar
Parable of the Pipeline	Burke Hedges
Questions Are the Answer	Allan Pease
The Magic of Thinking BIG	David Schwartz
Skill With People	Les Giblin
Positive Personality Profiles	Robert Rohm
What To Say When You Talk To Yourself	Shad Helmstetter

Recommended Listening

Title:	Speaker:
It's Not Over Till You Win	Les Brown
The Strangest Secret	Earl Nightingale
Unlimited Power	Anthony Robbins: